D0924084

of the World, Part II

nnas • Grasslands • Mountains a

Draw · Write NOW ®

by
Marie Hablitzel
and
Kim Stitzer

*A Drawing and
Handwriting
Course for Kids!*

Barker Cree sbo, Washington

Dedicated to...

...Virginia Crockett and Community Christian School.
I have enjoyed drawing with you! — M.H.

...Judy Richardson — K.S.

The text on the handwriting pages is set in a custom
font created from Marie Hablitzel's handwriting.
The drawings are done using Prismacolor pencils
outlined with a black PaperMate FLAIR!® felt tip pen.

BARKER CREEK

Published by Barker Creek Publishing, Inc.
P.O. Box 2610 • Poulsbo, WA 98370-2610
800•692•5833 FAX: 360•613•2542
barkercreek.com

Book layout by Judy Richardson
Printed in Hong Kong

Library of Congress Catalog Card Number: 93-73893

Publisher's Cataloging in Publication Data:
Hablitzel, Marie, 1920 -
Draw•Write•Now®, Book Eight: A drawing and handwriting course for kids!
(eighth in series)
Summary: A collection of drawing and handwriting lessons for children. **Book Eight** focuses on Grassland, Mountain & Desert Animals. Eighth book in the **Draw•Write•Now®** series. — 1st ed.
1. Drawing — Technique — Juvenile Literature. 2. Drawing — Study and Teaching (Elementary). 3. Penmanship. 4. Grassland Animals — Juvenile Literature. 5. Mountain Animals — Juvenile Literature. 6. Desert Animals — Juvenile Literature. 7. Cartography — Juvenile Literature. 8. Map Drawing — Juvenile Literature. 9. Animals — Juvenile Literature. 10. Africa — Juvenile Literature. I. Stitzer, Kim, 1956 -   , coauthor. II. Title.
741.2   [372.6] — dc 19

ISBN: 0-9639307-8-8

Second Printing

About this book...

For most children, drawing is their first form of written communication. Long before they master the alphabet and sentence syntax, children express themselves creatively on paper through line and color.

As children mature, their imaginations often race ahead of their drawing skills. By teaching them to see complex objects as combinations of simple shapes and encouraging them to develop their fine-motor skills through regular practice, they can better record the images they see so clearly in their minds.

This book contains a collection of beginning drawing lessons and text for practicing handwriting. These lessons were developed by a teacher who saw her second-grade students becoming increasingly frustrated with their drawing efforts and disenchanted with repetitive handwriting drills.

For more than 30 years, Marie Hablitzel refined what eventually became a daily drawing and handwriting curriculum. Marie's premise was simple — drawing and handwriting require many of the same skills. And, regular practice in a supportive environment is the key to helping children develop

Coauthors Marie Hablitzel (left) and her daughter, Kim Stitzer

their technical skills, self-confidence and creativity. As a classroom teacher, Marie intertwined her daily drawing and handwriting lessons with math, science, social studies, geography, reading and creative writing. She wove an educational tapestry that hundreds of children have found challenging, motivating — and fun!

Although Marie is now retired, her drawing and handwriting lessons continue to be used in the classroom. With the assistance of her daughter, Kim Stitzer, Marie shares more than 150 of her lessons in the eight-volume *Draw•Write•Now®* series.

In *Draw•Write•Now®*, *Book One*, children explore life on a farm, kids and critters and storybook characters. *Books Two* through *Six* feature topics as diverse as Christopher Columbus, the weather, Native Americans, the polar regions, young Abraham Lincoln, beaver ponds and life in the sea. In *Draw•Write•Now®*, *Books Seven and Eight*, children circle the globe while learning about animals of the world.

We hope your children and students enjoy these lessons as much as ours have!

— *Carolyn Hurst, Publisher*

Look for these books in the *Draw•Write•Now,®* series...

For additional information call 1-800-692-5833
or visit barkercreek.com

Table of Contents

A table of contents is like a map. It guides you to the places you want to visit in a book. Pick a subject you want to draw, then turn to the page listed beside the picture.

For more information on the *Draw•Write•Now*® series, see page 3.

For suggestions on how to use this book, see page 6.

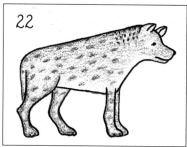

Savanna Animals Page 9

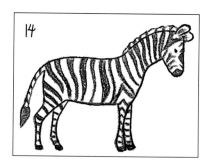

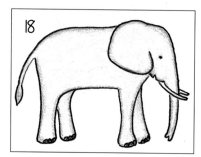
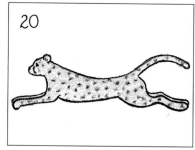
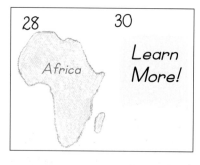

Grassland Animals

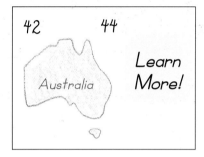
Mountain and Desert Animals

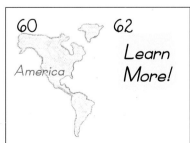
Teaching Tips

A few tips to get started...

This is a book for children and their parents, teachers and caregivers. Although most young people can complete the lessons in this book quite successfully on their own, a little help and encouragement from a caring adult can go a long way toward building a child's self-confidence, creativity and technical skills.

Frog by Brendan Williamson, age 7
from Draw•Write•Now®, Book Six

The following outline contains insights from the 30-plus years the authors have worked with the material in this book. Realizing that no two children or classrooms are alike, the authors encourage you to modify these lessons to best suit the needs of your child or classroom. Each *Draw•Write•Now®* lesson includes five parts:

1. Introduce the subject
2. Draw the subject
3. Draw the background
4. Practice handwriting
5. Color the drawing

As presented here, each child will need a pencil, an eraser, drawing paper, penmanship paper and either crayons, color pencils or felt tip markers to complete a lesson.

1. Introduce the Subject

Begin the lesson by generating interest in the subject with a story, discussion, poem, photograph or song. The questions on the illustrated notes scattered throughout this book are examples of how interest can be built along a related theme. Answers to these questions and the titles of several theme-related books are on pages 30, 44 and 62.

2. Draw the Subject

Have the children draw with a pencil. Encourage them to draw lightly because some lines (shown as dashed lines on the drawing lessons) will need to be erased. Point out the shapes and lines in the subject as the children work through the lesson. Help the children see that complex objects can be viewed as combinations of lines and simple shapes.

Help the children be successful! Show them how to position the first step on their papers in an appropriate size. Initially, the children may find some shapes difficult to draw. If they do, provide a pattern for them to trace, or draw the first step for them. Once they fine-tune their skills and build their self-confidence, their ability and creativity will take over. For lesson-specific drawing tips and suggestions, refer to *Teaching Tips* on pages 63–64.

3. Draw the Background

Encourage the children to express their creativity and imaginations in the backgrounds they add to their pictures. Add to their creative libraries by demonstrating various ways to draw trees, horizons and other details. Point out background details in the drawings in this book, illustrations from other books, photographs and works of art.

Encourage the children to draw their world by looking for basic shapes and lines in the things they see around them. Ask them to draw from their imaginations by using their developing skills.

4. Practice Handwriting

In place of drills — rows of e's, r's and so on — it is often useful and more motivating to have children write complete sentences when they practice their handwriting. When the focus is on handwriting rather than spelling or vocabulary enrichment, use simple words that the children can easily read and spell. Begin by writing each sentence with the simple words that the children can easily read and spell. Begin by writing each sentence with the children, demonstrating how individual letters are formed and stressing proper spacing. Start slowly. One or two sentences may be challenging enough in the beginning. Once the children are consistently forming their letters correctly, encourage them to work at their own pace.

Hermit Crab by Sam Johnson, age 6
from Draw•Write•Now®, Book Six

There are many ways to adapt these lessons for use with your child or classroom. For example, you may want to replace the authors' text with your own words. You may want to let the children compose sentences to describe their drawings or answer the theme-related questions found throughout the book. You may prefer to replace the block alphabet used in this book with a cursive, D'Nealian® or other alphabet style. If you are unfamiliar with the various alphabet styles used for teaching handwriting, consult your

African Elephant by Kirsten Wabbel, age 8
from Draw•Write•Now®, Book Eight

local library. A local elementary school may also be able to recommend an appropriate alphabet style and related resource materials.

5. Color the Picture

Children enjoy coloring their own drawings. The beautiful colors, however, often cover the details they have so carefully drawn in pencil. To preserve their efforts, you may want to have the children trace their pencil lines with black crayons or fine-tipped felt markers.

Crayons — When they color with crayons, have the children outline their drawings with a black crayon *after* they have colored their pictures (the black crayon may smear if they do their outlining first).

Color Pencils — When they color with color pencils, have the children outline their drawings with a felt tip marker *before* they color their drawings.

Felt Tip Markers — When they color with felt tip

Angler Fish by Luke Thoresen, age 7
from Draw•Write•Now®, Book Six

markers, have the children outline their drawings with a black marker *after* they have colored their pictures.

Your comments are appreciated!
How are you sharing Draw•Write•Now® with your children or students? The authors would appreciate hearing from you. Write to Marie Hablitzel and Kim Stitzer, c/o Barker Creek Publishing, Inc., P.O. Box 2610, Poulsbo, WA 98370, USA or visit us at barkercreek.com.

Handwriting is an Art!

Practice Handwriting
Carefully

1. Sit up straight.
2. Hold your pencil correctly.
3. Use the paper guidelines.
4. Form each letter carefully.
5. Space the words evenly.
6. Practice daily.

The more you practice,
the better your writing will look!

Savanna Animals

Llanos

Savanna

Cerrado

Rangeland

Living on the Tropical Grasslands of the World

Giraffes live in Africa on the grasslands.

Giraffes live on the savanna.
The weather is always warm.
Giraffes reach for tree branches.
They eat the leaves.

What is a savanna?

Giraffe

Question answered on page 30

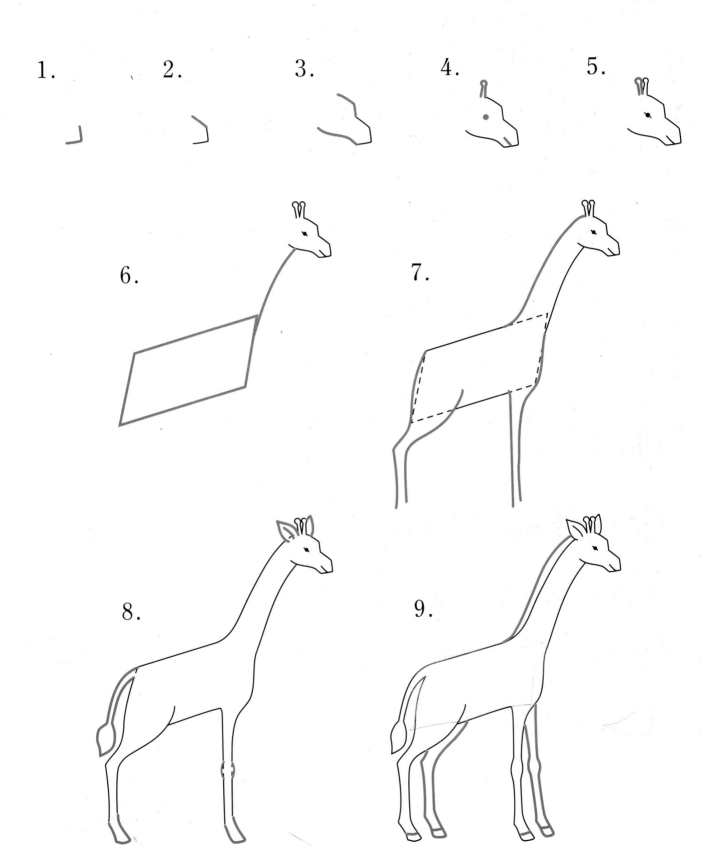

1.   2.   3.   4.   5.

6.   7.

8.   9.

Hippopotamus

Question answered on page 30

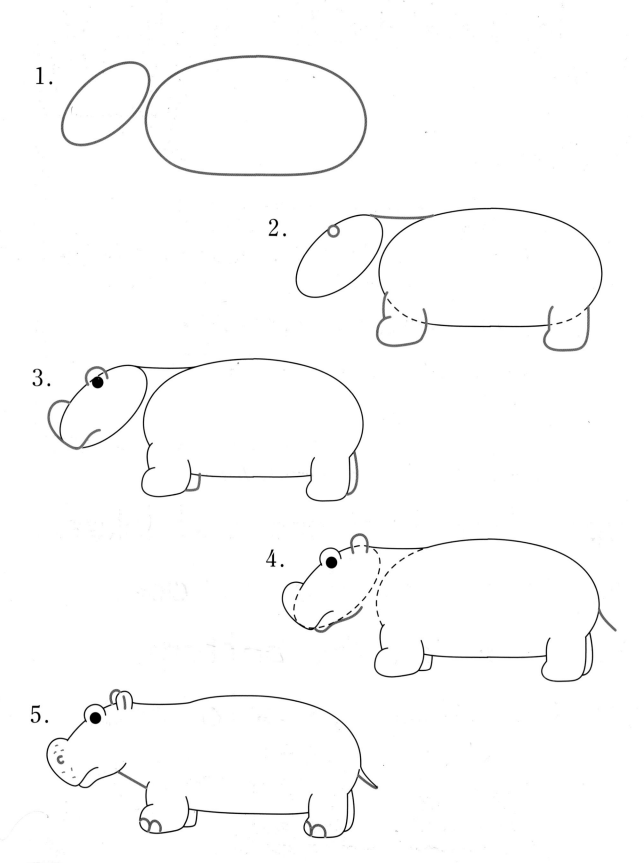

1.

2.

3.

4.

5.

Hippopotami live in Africa on the grasslands and forests.

Hippos live in rivers and lakes.
They float at the surface.
They walk on the bottom.
At night they go onto land.

Why do hippos leave the water at night?

Zebras live in Africa on the grasslands and forests.

Zebras gallop across the plains.
They graze on grasses.
Water holes dot the plains.
Zebras stop to drink at them.

What is a water hole?

Zebra

Question answered on page 30

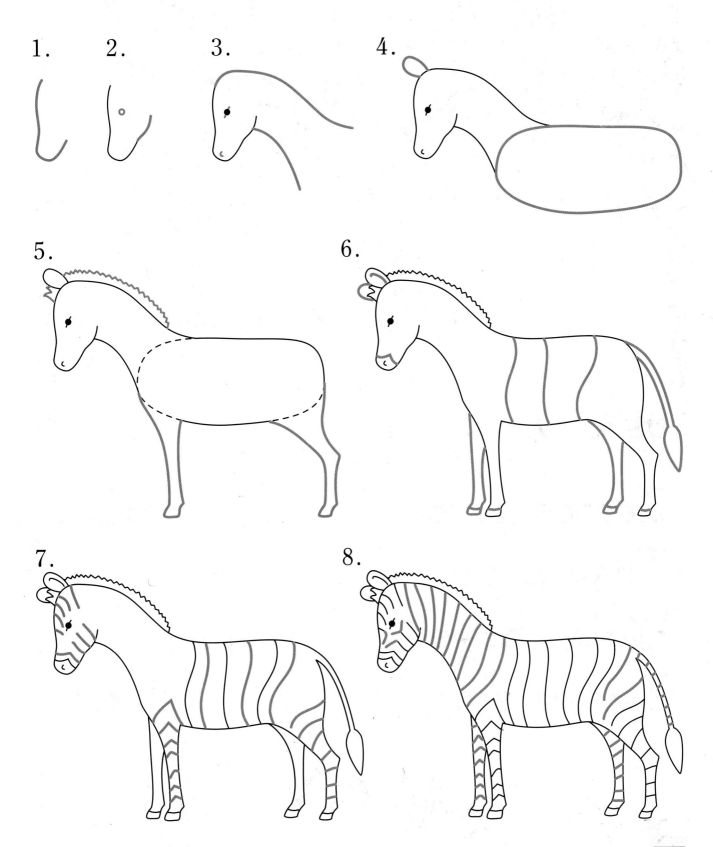

1.
2.
3.
4.
5.
6.
7.
8.

Lion

Question answered on page 30

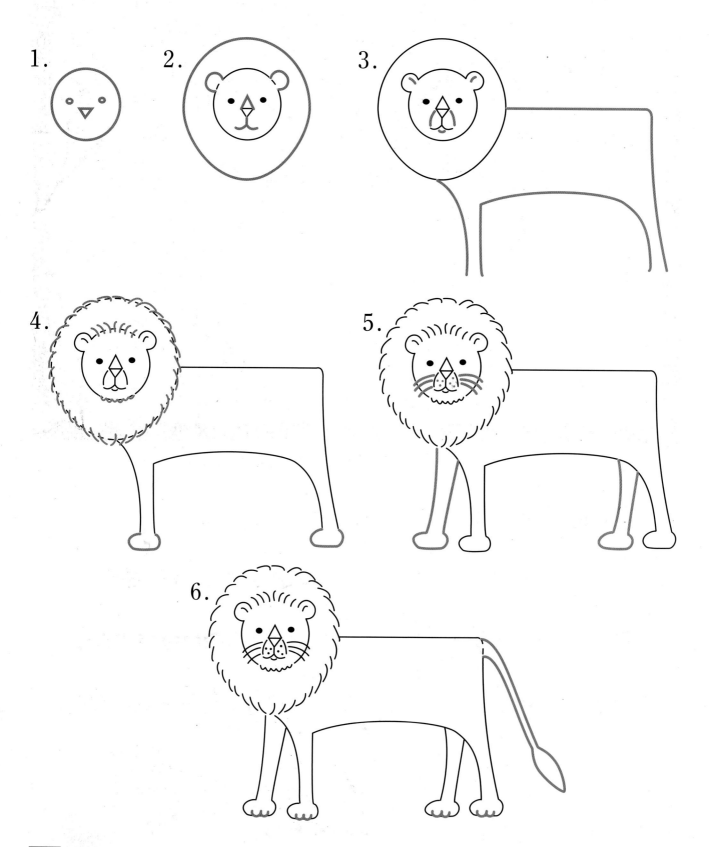

1.

2.

3.

4.

5.

6.

Lions live in Africa on the grasslands and open forests.

Lions are hunters.

They wait near water holes.

Other animals drink carefully.

They know lions may be near.

Do all lions have manes?

African elephants live on grasslands. Another species of elephant lives in Asia.

Elephants cross the savanna.

They travel in a herd.

The elephants walk single file.

The same path is used each year.

How many miles do elephants travel?

Elephant

Question answered on page 30

African Elephant

1.

(fold or lightly drawn line)

2.

3.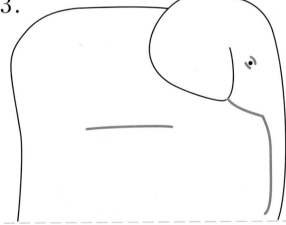

4.

5.

6.

Cheetah

Question answered on page 30

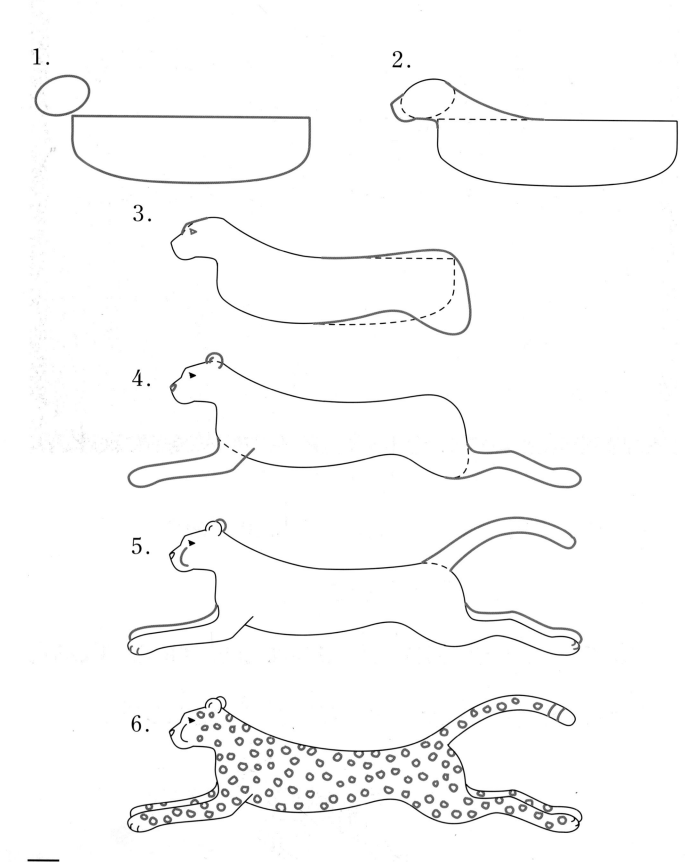

1.

2.

3.

4.

5.

6.

Cheetahs live in Africa and Asia on the grasslands.

The cheetah is a hunter.

It chases its prey.

Many grassland animals are fast.

The cheetah is the fastest.

When can a gazelle run faster than a cheetah?

Hyenas live in Africa and western Asia on the grasslands and deserts.

The hyena is a strong animal.
It has powerful shoulders.
It crushes bones with its jaws.
It can run many miles.

Are hyenas and dogs related?

African Wild Dog

Spotted Hyena

1.

2.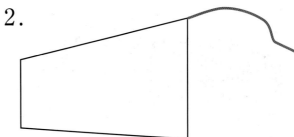

3.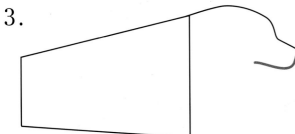

4.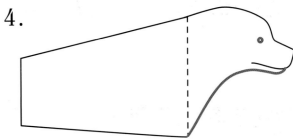

5.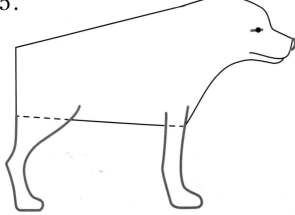

6.

7.

8.

Ostrich

Question answered on page 30

1.

2.

3.

4.

5.

Ostriches live in Africa and Asia on the grasslands and sandy brushlands.

The ostrich needs little water.

It is the largest bird in the world.

The ostrich runs very fast.

It does not fly.

How tall is an ostrich?

Rhinoceroses live in Africa and Asia on the grasslands and forests.

Rhinos live near pools and rivers.
They wallow in the mud.
Rhinos run and move quickly.
They can even jump!

Why do rhinos wallow in the mud?

Flamingo

Question answered on page 30

White Rhino

1.

2.

3.

4.

5.

6.

7.

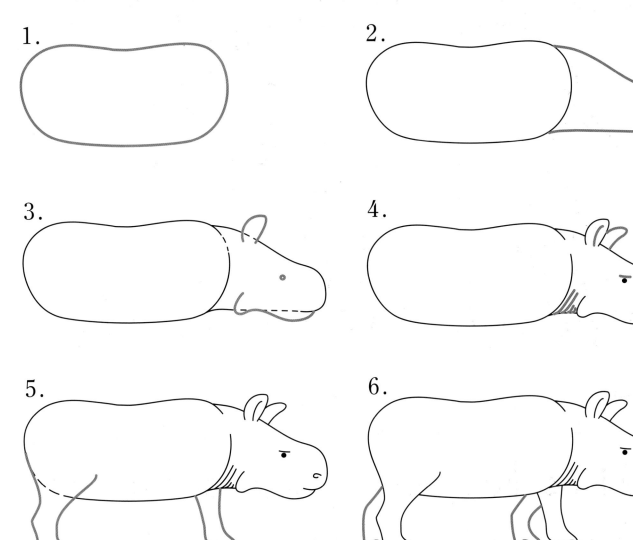

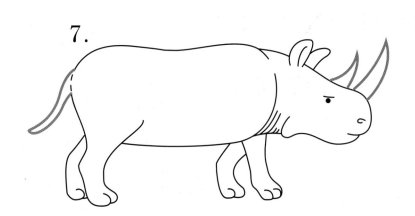

Savannas of the World

Less rain falls on the savannas than on the forests, but there is enough rain for grasses and wildflowers to grow. Some trees grow on the savanna, but they must survive the long, dry season.

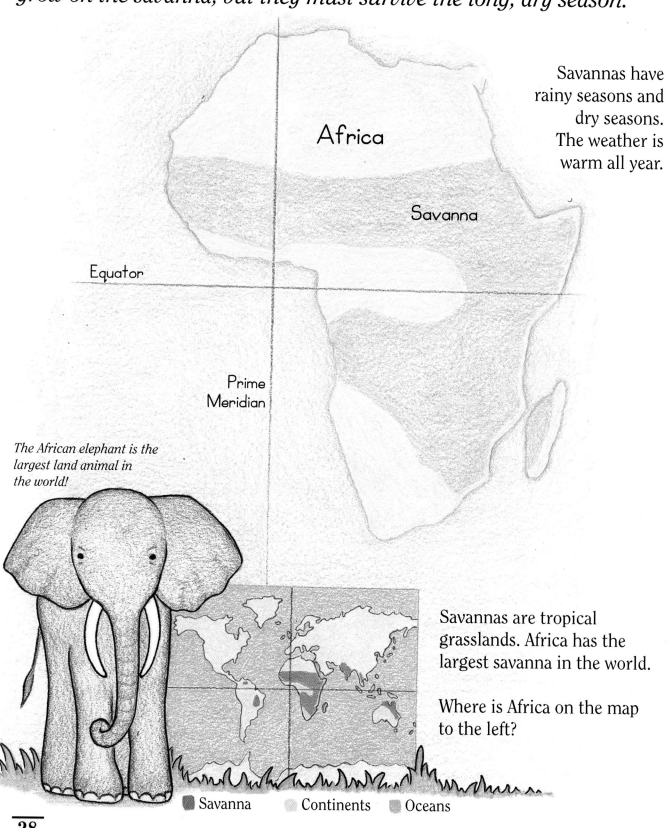

Savannas have rainy seasons and dry seasons. The weather is warm all year.

Africa

Savanna

Equator

Prime Meridian

The African elephant is the largest land animal in the world!

Savannas are tropical grasslands. Africa has the largest savanna in the world.

Where is Africa on the map to the left?

■ Savanna   ■ Continents   ■ Oceans

Draw a map of Africa.

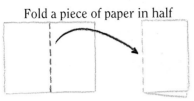

Fold a piece of paper in half

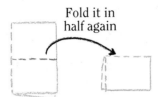

Fold it in half again

Unfold the paper

1.
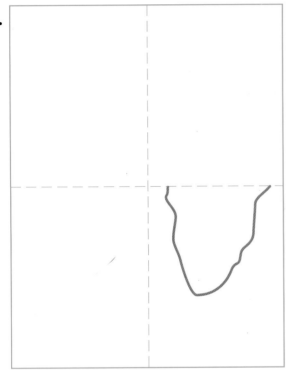

2.
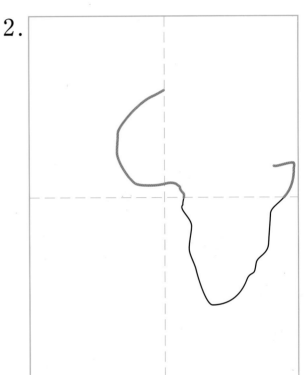

3.
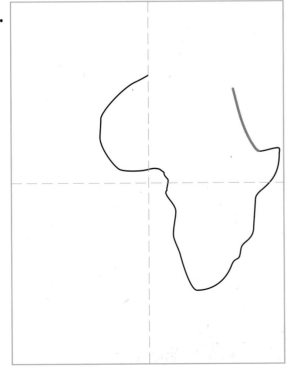

4.
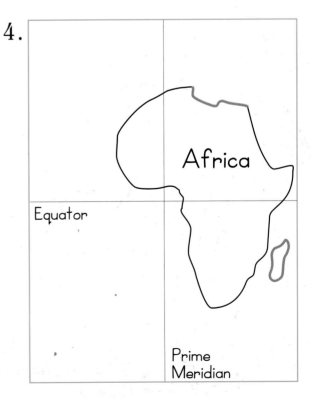

Africa

Equator

Prime Meridian

Learn more about savanna animals . . .

WHAT IS A SAVANNA? Page 10

A savanna is a grassland — a vast plain with a variety of grasses — which is located near the equator. Visit the largest savanna in the world with HERE IS THE AFRICAN SAVANNA *written by Madeleine Dunphy, illustrated by Tom Leonard, published by Hyperion, 1999.*

WHY DO HIPPOS LEAVE THE WATER AT NIGHT? Page 13

Hippos live near the equator, where the sun's rays hit directly onto the earth. A hippopotamus gets uncomfortable in the sun, much like people do when they get sunburned. Rather than exposing themselves to the sun, hippos rest in rivers or lakes. At dusk, they leave the river and graze on grass throughout the night. An African tale provides a funny perspective on this in HOT HIPPO *by Mwenye Hadithi, illustrated by Adrienne Kennaway, published by Little, Brown & Company, 1986.*

WHAT IS A WATER HOLE? Page 14

Savannas have rainy seasons and dry seasons. A water hole is a low place in the land which collects water during the rainy season. During the dry season, the water gradually evaporates and the water hole shrinks or dries up. See how the African savanna changes with the seasons in TREE OF LIFE *written and illustrated by Barbara Bash, published by Sierra Club Books, 1989.*

DO ALL LIONS HAVE MANES? Page 17

Only the adult male lion has a long mane around its face. With his loud roar and strength, the male protects the family, but the female lion is the great hunter. Get a view of Africa from an artist's perspective in SAFARI *written and illustrated by Robert Bateman, published by Little, Brown & Company, 1998.*

HOW MANY MILES DO ELEPHANTS TRAVEL? Page 18

If unrestricted by human farms or villages, African elephants can travel hundreds of miles each year. Today, most elephants live in nature reserves and their migrations are restricted. Still, they move from one feeding ground to the next, following a familiar loop on the reserve. Learn more with THEY WALK THE EARTH *by Seymour Simon, illustrated by Elsa Warnick, published by Harcourt, 2000.*

WHEN CAN A GAZELLE RUN FASTER THAN A CHEETAH? Page 21

A gazelle will outrun a cheetah if the cheetah doesn't catch it within 30 seconds. At a top speed of up to 70 miles per hour the cheetah maintains its sprint for only a short time, then drops in exhaustion. Observe the chase with CHEETAH *written and illustrated by Taylor Morrison, published by Henry Holt, 1998. Then, read the story of an orphaned cheetah raised by a family in* HOW IT WAS WITH DOOMS *written and illustrated by Xan Hopcraft and Carol Cawthra Hopcraft, published by Aladdin, 1997.*

ARE HYENAS AND DOGS RELATED? Page 22

No, hyenas look similar to dogs but they are not related. The closest relative to the hyena is the aardwolf. See how the hyena lives with AFRICAN WILDLIFE, *written by Barbara Bach and Stephen Krasemann, photographed by Stephen Krasemann, published by NorthWord Press, 1998. (Warning! The lions and cheetahs are hunting in a few of the photographs. The images may be too graphic for some people.)*

HOW TALL IS AN OSTRICH? Page 25

A male ostrich is eight feet tall — that's taller than a basketball player — and a newly hatched ostrich is the size of a chicken! Learn about the world's largest bird and other African birds with THE BIRD ATLAS *by Barbara Taylor, illustrated by Richard Orr, published by Dorling Kindersley, 1993.*

WHY DO RHINOS WALLOW IN THE MUD? Page 26

Like many savanna animals, rhinos coat their skin with mud for protection from sunburn and insects. Surprisingly, rhinos are quick and nimble, even with their large horns and big, leathery bodies. See WHOSE BOTTOM IS THIS? *written and photographed by Wayne Lynch, published by Whitecap, 2000.*

Grassland Animals

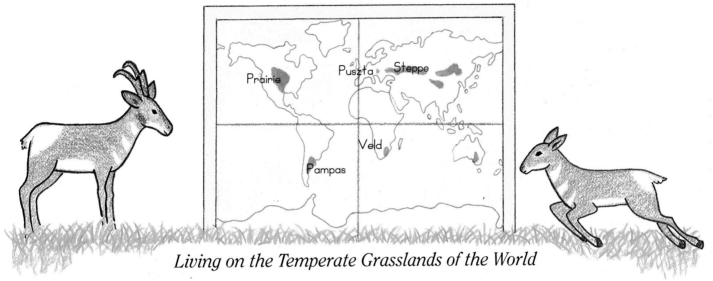

Living on the Temperate Grasslands of the World

Horses live all over the world. Once, they lived only on the grasslands of Europe and Asia.

Horses gallop across the steppes.

They graze on the grass.

Long ago, all horses were wild.

Today, most horses are tame.

What are the steppes?

Horse

Question answered on page 44

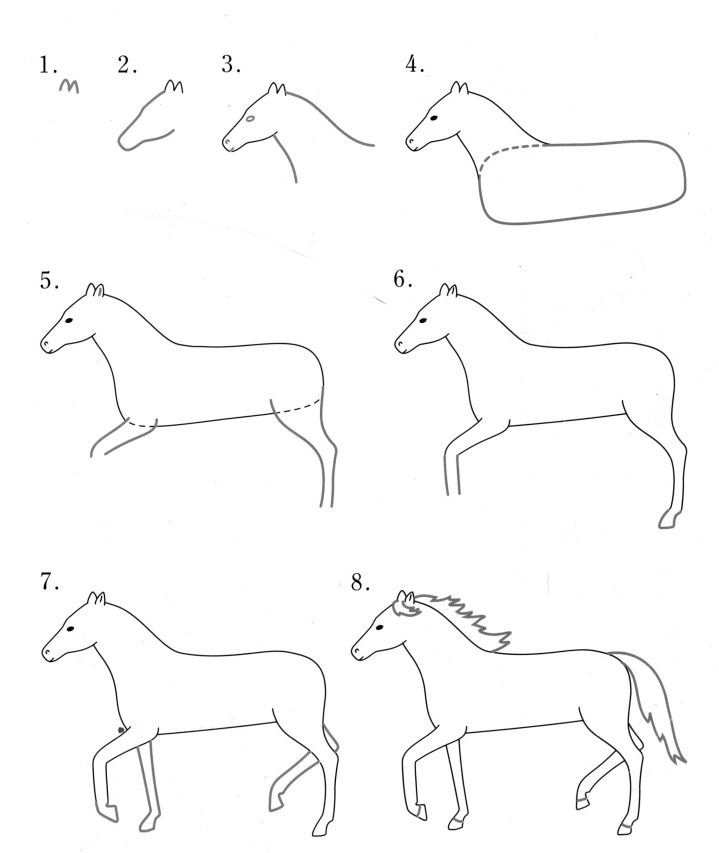

1.

2.

3.

4.

5.

6.

7.

8.

Anteater

Question answered on page 44

Giant Anteater

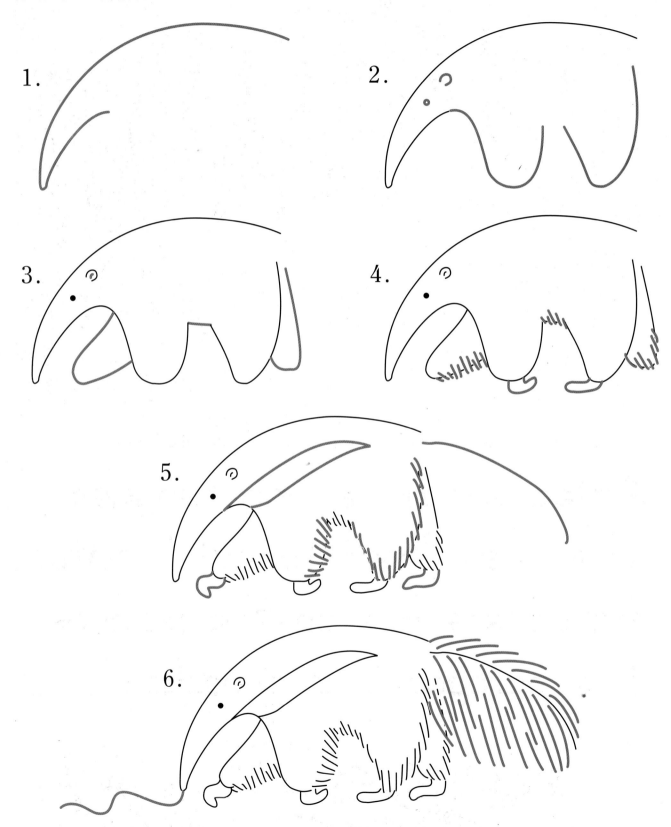

Anteaters live in South America on the grasslands and forests.

Anteaters have long tongues.
They use them to catch ants.
Anteaters live on the pampas.
The pampas is a grassland.

What other insects live on the pampas?

Armadillos live in southern North America and in South America on grasslands and forests.

The armadillo lives on the prairie.
Armor covers its body.
It has bony plates on its back.
Tough skin covers the plates.

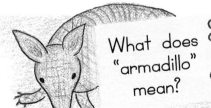

What does "armadillo" mean?

Armadillo

Question answered on page 44

Nine-banded Armadillo

1.

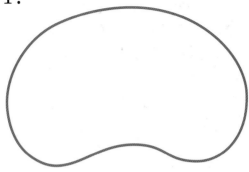

2.

3.

4.

5.

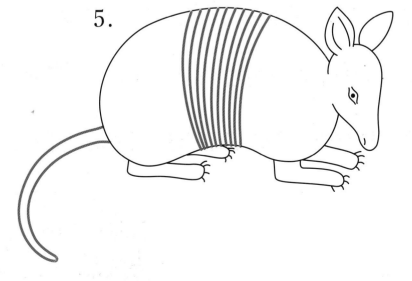

Prairie Dog

Question answered on page 44

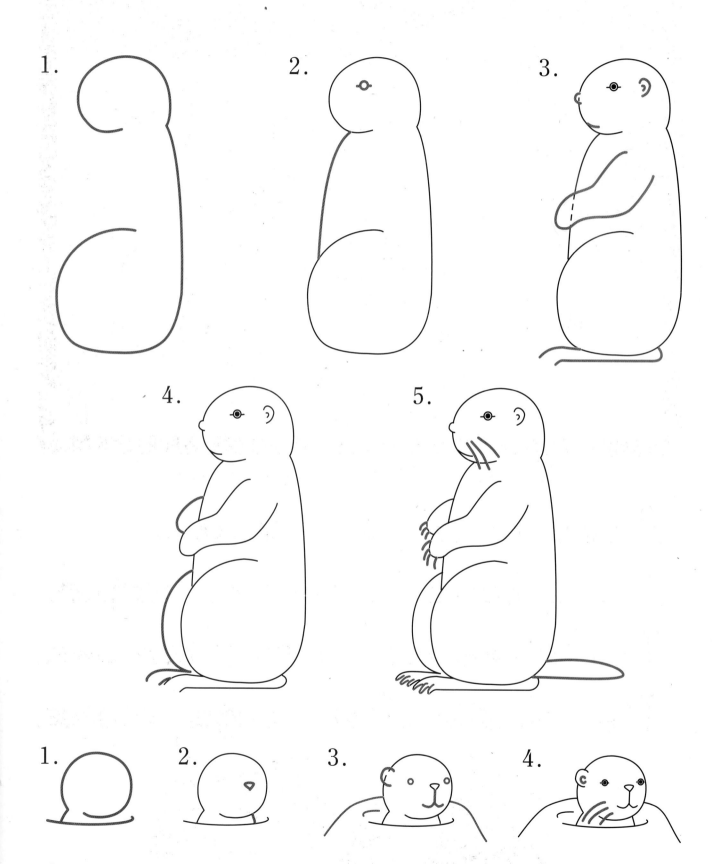

1.

2.

3.

4.

5.

1.

2.

3.

4.

Prairie dogs live in North America on the grasslands.

Prairie dogs live in groups.

A dog barks to warn of danger.

The others run to their burrows.

They whistle after danger passes.

Is the prairie dog really a dog?

Pronghorns live in North America on the grasslands.

Pronghorns are hard to catch.
They sprint across the plains.
Coyotes chase after them.
The prairie is their home.

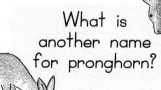

What is another name for pronghorn?

Question answered on page 44

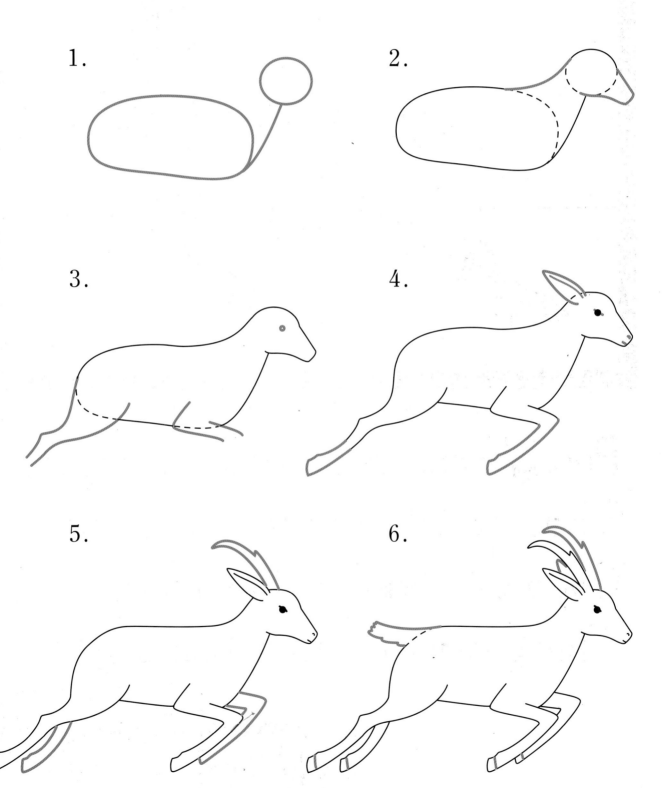

1.

2.

3.

4.

5.

6.

Temperate Grasslands of the World

Less rain falls on the grasslands than the forests, but there is enough rain for grasses and wildflowers to grow. Very few trees grow on the grasslands, except along rivers and stream.

Australia's tropical grassland is called the rangeland. It is like the African savanna.

Tropical Grassland or Rangeland

Australia

The temperate grasslands of Australia are mostly farmlands. They are like the North American prairie.

Temperate Grasslands

Temperate grasslands have cold winters and hot summers.

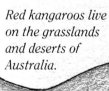
Red kangaroos live on the grasslands and deserts of Australia.

Where is Australia on the map to the left?

● Temperate Grasslands ▨ Continents ▨ Oceans

Draw a map of Australia.

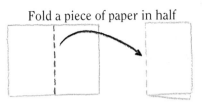
Fold a piece of paper in half

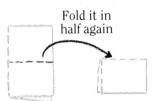
Fold it in half again

Unfold the paper

1.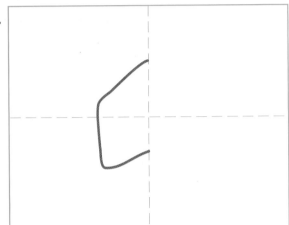

2.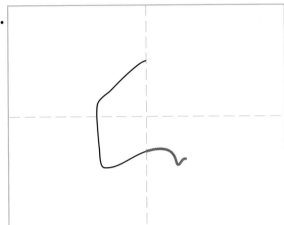

3.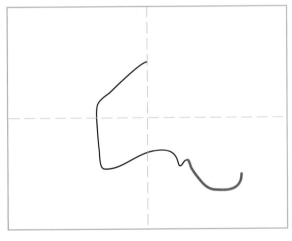

4.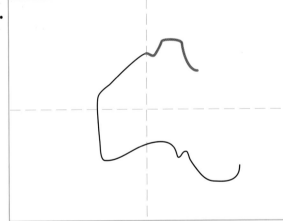

5.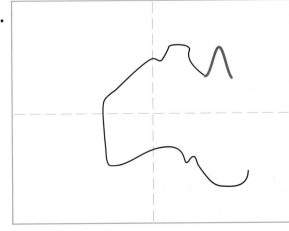

6.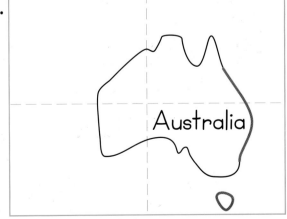

Australia

Learn more about grassland animals . . .

WHAT ARE THE STEPPES?   Page 32

The steppes are treeless, grassy plains which stretch across eastern Europe and central Asia. This grassland is the home of the true wild horse. Learn the history of the horse with THE TRUE-OR-FALSE BOOK OF HORSES *by Patricia Lauber, illustrated by Rosalyn Schanzer, published by HarperCollins, 2000.*

WHAT OTHER INSECTS LIVE ON THE PAMPAS?   Page 35

Like all grasslands, the wide open pampas is home to large quantities and varieties of insects: termites, beetles, ants . . . and more! See how insects are distributed on our planet with ATLAS OF INSECTS *by Michael Tweedie, published by John Day Company, 1974.*

WHAT DOES "ARMADILLO" MEAN?   Page 36

"Armadillo" means "little armored one" in Spanish. The armadillo has warrior-like armor and claws, but it is a very gentle, timid animal. Travel along with the curious and inquisitive character in ARMADILLO FROM AMARILLO *written and illustrated by Lynne Cherry, published by Harcourt Brace, 1994.*

IS THE PRAIRIE DOG REALLY A DOG?   Page 39

No, the prairie dog is a rodent, like a squirrel, but was named for its shrill bark which is similar to a dog's bark. Not only do prairie dogs bark, they yip and whistle. Learn more about this social animal with PRAIRIE DOGS *by Emery Bernhard, illustrated by Durga Bernhard, published by Harcourt Brace, 1997. The black-footed ferret likes to live near a prairie dog town. See why with* PHANTOM OF THE PRAIRIE *by Jonathan London, illustrated by Barbara Bash, published by Sierra Club Books, 1998.*

WHAT IS ANOTHER NAME FOR PRONGHORN?   Page 40

"Antelope" is what many people call the pronghorn, but antelope do not live in North America — they live on the savannas of Africa and Asia. Whatever its name, the pronghorn is in the record books as the second fastest animal in the world! See North America's plains in IF YOU'RE NOT FROM THE PRAIRIE *by Dave Bouchard, illustrated by Henry Ripplinger, published by Atheneum, 1995.*

COMPARE THE SIMILARITIES AND DIFFERENCES OF TEMPERATE AND TROPICAL GRASSLANDS:

The two types of grasslands are different because of their locations on this earth. Latitude and altitude make the difference in whether a place is warm or cool. Generally, it is warm at the equator and at sea level, and cooler near the poles and on tall mountains. See a variety of landscapes at various latitudes in ONE DAY IN MARCH *by Marilyn Singer, illustrated by Frané Lessac, published by HarperCollins, 2000.*

TEMPERATE GRASSLANDS:

A variety of grasses grow on grasslands. These plains are treeless, except along rivers or streams. Grasslands have distinct winter and summer seasons and are home to large grazing animals, like bison and horses. Most temperate grasslands have been converted to farm or ranch lands.

TROPICAL GRASSLANDS:

A variety of grasses grow on tropical grasslands. Trees are scattered across the landscape. The tropical grasslands are warm year-round, with rainy seasons and dry seasons. The largest, tallest and fastest land animals live on the African savanna. Much of the world's tropical grasslands have been converted to farm or ranch land.

GRASSLAND LOCATIONS:
Africa — Veld
Europe — The Steppes
Asia — The Steppes
North America — Prairie
South America — Pampas
Australia — Murray River region

TROPICAL GRASSLAND LOCATIONS:
Africa — Savanna
South America — Ilanos and Cerrado
Australia — Rangelands
Asia — grasslands of India and Indonesia

Mountain and Desert Animals

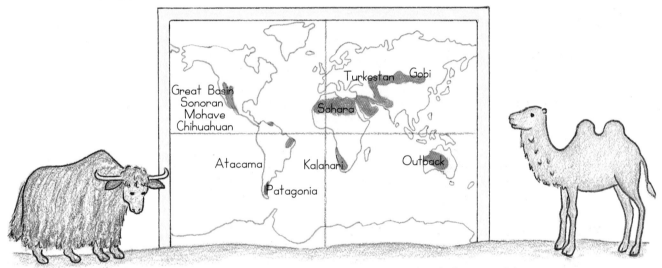

Living on the Snow-Capped Mountains of the World
Living in the Deserts and Brushlands of the World

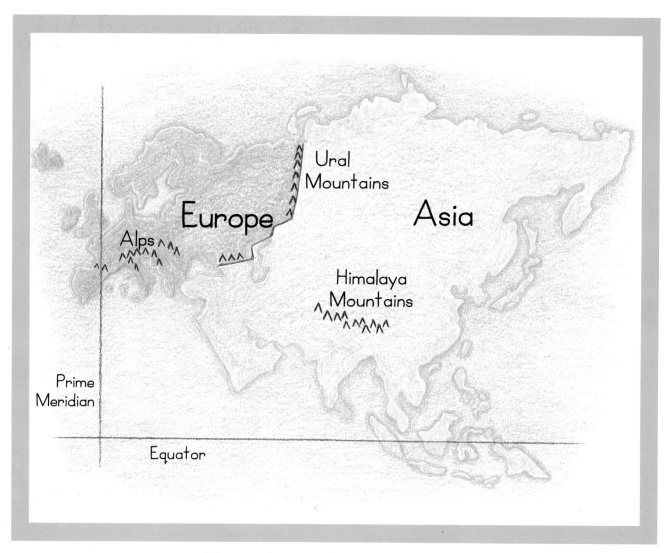

The continents of Europe and Asia.

The mountains of Asia are huge.
They are the tallest in the world.
Animals migrate to mountains.
Some stay all year.

Why are Europe
and Asia two
continents?

Europe and Asia

Question answered on page 62

Fold a piece of paper in half

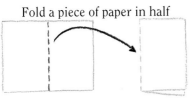

Fold it in half again

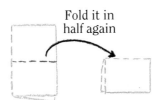

Unfold the paper

1.
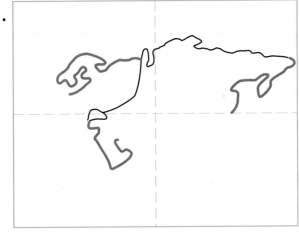

2.
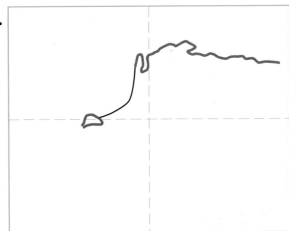

3.
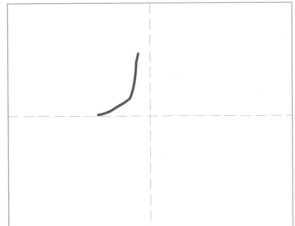

4.
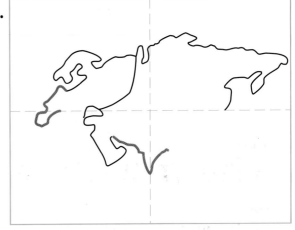

5.
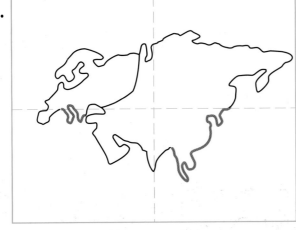

6.
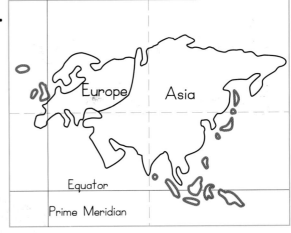

Europe   Asia

Equator

Prime Meridian

Yak

Question answered on page 62

1.

2.

3.

4.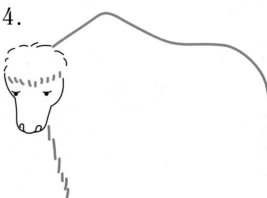

5.

6.

7.

Yaks live in Asia in the Himalaya Mountains and the highlands of Tibet.

Yaks live on tall mountains.

They graze on herbs and grasses.

The air is cold near the peaks.

Yaks have thick, warm fur.

Why is the air cold near the top of a mountain?

Golden eagles live on the mountains of Europe, Asia, northern Africa and North America.

Golden eagles live in the mountains.
They build nests on cliffs.
Eagles soar across the sky.
They hunt small animals.

What is an alpine tundra?

1.

2.

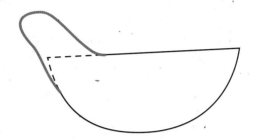

3.

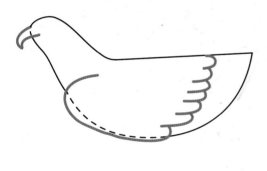

4.

5.

6.

Llama

Question answered on page 62

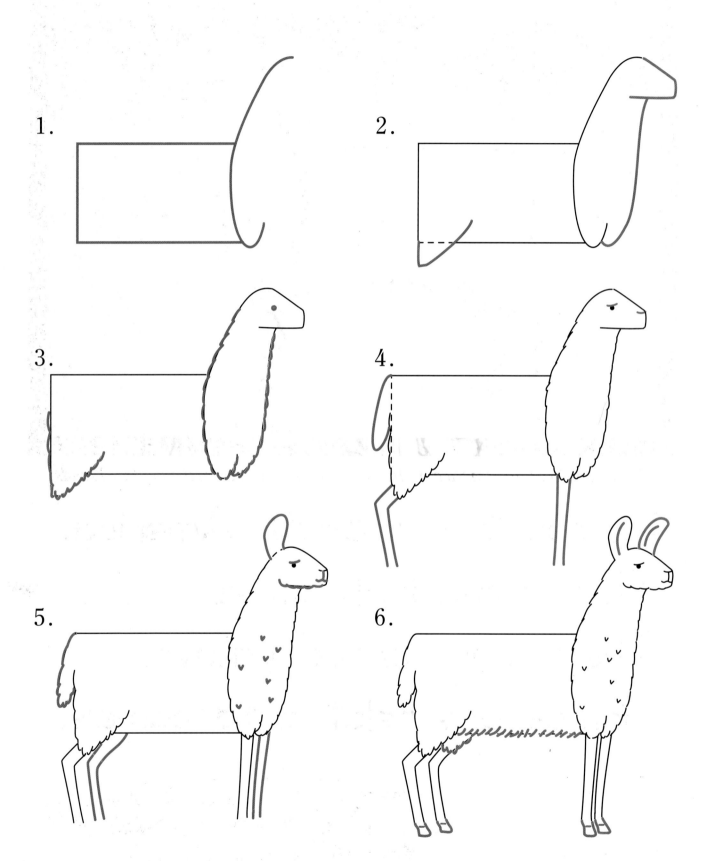

1.

2.

3.

4.

5.

6.

Llamas live in South America in the Andes Mountains and on the dry brushlands.

Llamas live in South America.

They climb high slopes.

They cross broad valleys.

Llamas are related to camels.

Vizcacha

Do llamas have humps like camels?

Cavy

Guinea Pig

Other South American animals

Camels live in Africa and Asia in deserts. The Dromedary lives in Africa and western Asia.

Camels travel far without food.
They get energy from fat.
It is in humps on their backs.
Camels can go without water, too.

one hump

two humps

How long can a camel go without a drink of water?

Dromedary Camel

Bactrian Camel

Question answered on page 62

Dromedary Camel

1.

2.

3.

4.

5.

6.

Thorny Lizard

Question answered on page 62

1.

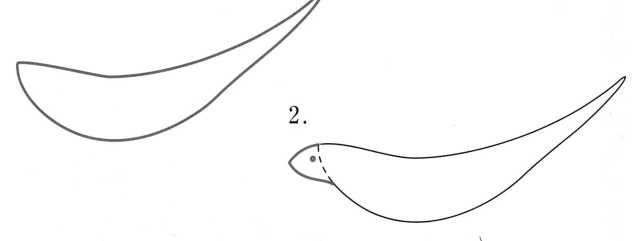

2.

3.

4.

5.

6.

Thorny lizards live in Australia in the deserts.

A thorny lizard can collect water.

Dew settles on its back.

The droplets run into grooves.

The grooves lead to its mouth.

How long is a thorny lizard?

Coyotes live in North America in deserts, grasslands, shrub lands and forests.

Coyotes chase small animals.
They are quick and clever.
Coyotes howl to each other.
The howls echo across valleys.

Where do coyotes sleep?

Coyote

Question answered on page 62

1.

2.

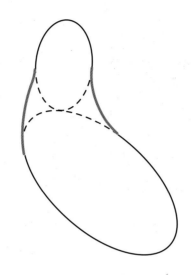

3.

4.

5.

6.

Deserts of the World

Very little rain falls on the deserts and brushlands of the world. Plants with small leaves and cacti grow in deserts and brushlands.

North America and South America have deserts and dry brushlands. Cacti grow in these deserts.

North America

Jackrabbits live in the deserts, southern grasslands and shrub lands of North America.

Equator

South America

Where is North America on the map to the left?

Where is South America?

Deserts   Continents   Oceans

Draw a map of North America.

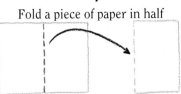 Fold a piece of paper in half

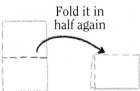 Fold it in half again

 Unfold the paper

1.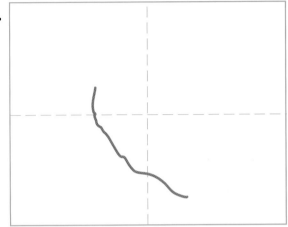

2.

3.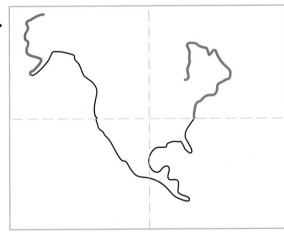

4.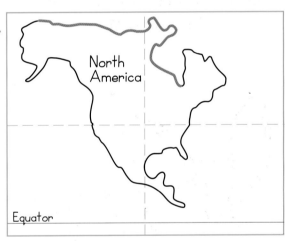

North America

Equator

Draw a map of South America.

1.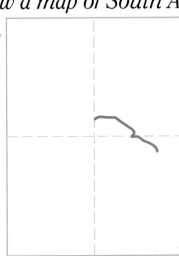

2.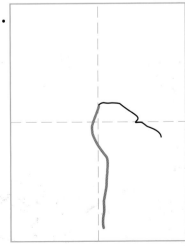

3.

Equator   South America

Learn more about mountain animals . . .

WHY ARE EUROPE AND ASIA TWO CONTINENTS? Page 46

Even though they are one land mass, Europe and Asia were named long ago
as two continents due to a natural boundary of mountain ranges, seas and deserts.
Learn about Europe and Asia's mountains and the world's other magnificent ranges with MOUNTAINS
by Seymour Simon, published by Morrow Junior, 1994.

WHY IS THE AIR COLD NEAR THE TOP OF A MOUNTAIN? Page 49

The higher the elevation, the cooler the air. So, land near mountain tops is colder than land near the sea.
The wild yak, with its heavy coat of fur and reliance on a diet of tender green plants, is perfectly suited for
the highlands. Like many mountain animals, it spends the winter months on the lower levels of the
mountain, then migrates to the higher levels in summer. Learn more with NATIONAL GEOGRAPHIC
BOOK OF MAMMALS, *published by National Geographic, 1998.*

WHAT IS AN ALPINE TUNDRA? Page 50

There are two tundra environments on earth, the alpine tundra and the Arctic tundra. The alpine tundra
is the area that extends from the treeline to the top of snow-covered mountains. The Arctic tundra is the
land surrounding the Arctic Ocean and North Pole. Tundra plants include grass, wildflowers, mosses and
lichens. During the short summer, many animals flock to the tundras to feed on the small, tender plants
which quickly sprout after the snow melts. Study the Arctic with DRAW•WRITE•NOW, BOOK FOUR *by*
Marie Hablitzel and Kim Stitzer, published by Barker Creek, 1998. Learn about the alpine tundra with
ONE DAY IN THE ALPINE TUNDRA *by Jean Craighead George, illustrated by Walter Gaffney-Kessell,*
published by Scholastic, 1984.

DO LLAMAS HAVE HUMPS LIKE CAMELS? Page 53

No, only the camel has humps. The llama's distinguishing feature is its large, strong
lungs. The air in high elevations contains much less oxygen than air at sea level. So,
animals and people who live at such heights have remarkably strong lungs. Learn about
life in the Andes Mountains with THIS PLACE IS HIGH *by Vicki Cobb, illustrated by*
Barbara Lavallee, published by Walker, 1989.

Learn more about desert animals . . .

HOW LONG CAN A CAMEL GO WITHOUT A DRINK OF WATER? Page 54

A camel can go one week without a drink and one month without food. There are two species of camels.
The camels with one hump live in the hot deserts of Africa and western Asia. The camels with two humps
live in the high, cool deserts of Asia and have heavier coats of fur. Both types of camels are used by people
to move heavy loads across the deserts — even today, with the availability of motor vehicles. Follow the
story of a boy who becomes lost while riding across the desert in ALI, CHILD OF THE DESERT *by Jonathan*
London, illustrated by Ted Lewin, published by Lothrop, Lee & Shepard, 1997.

HOW LONG IS A THORNY LIZARD? Page 57

The slow-moving Thorny is between four and six inches long. The true name of this
lizard is "Thorny Devil". Sharp spikes cover its body for protection, but it is a harmless
lizard — even though its name implies otherwise. Learn about the harsh environment
it lives in with DESERTS *by Seymour Simon, published by Morrow Junior, 1997.*

WHERE DO COYOTES SLEEP? Page 58

Coyotes sleep during the daytime in underground burrows. Like most desert
animals, the coyote is active at night when it is cool. See the coyote in action
with COYOTE AT PINON PLACE *by Deborah Dennard, illustrated by John*
Paul Genzo, published by Soundprints, 1999.

Teaching Tips

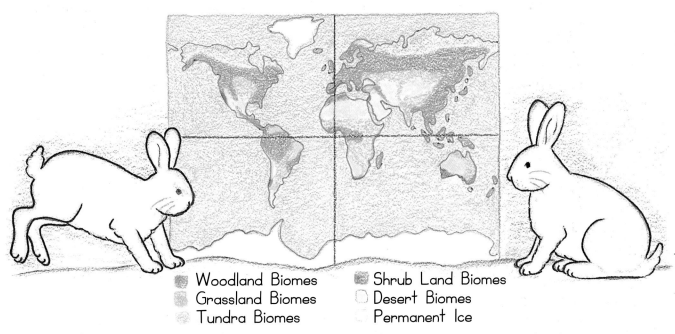

- 🟫 Woodland Biomes
- 🟩 Grassland Biomes
- 🟡 Tundra Biomes
- 🟥 Shrub Land Biomes
- ⬜ Desert Biomes
- ⬜ Permanent Ice

Biomes are large areas on earth where similar plants grow.

Woodland Biomes

TROPICAL FORESTS (Tropical Rain Forests, Mangrove Forests, Congo, Amazon) — Tropical forests have abundant rainfall and year-round warmth. Tall trees shade the forests.

TEMPERATE FORESTS (Broadleaf Forests, Coniferous Forests) — Temperate forests have distinct seasons and regular rainfall. In autumn, the broadleaf tree leaves are brilliant reds, oranges and golds.

■ Forests

Continents

Oceans

BOREAL FORESTS — (Tiaga, Siberia, Coniferous Forests) — Boreal forests have long, cold winters. They stretch across Europe, Asia and North America.

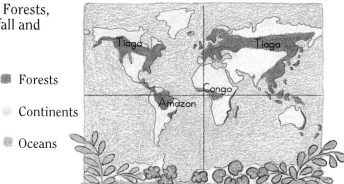

Find lessons on forest animals in *Draw•Write•Now®, Book Seven.*

Grassland Biomes

TROPICAL GRASSLANDS (Savannas, Llanos, Cerrado, Rangeland) — Tropical grasslands are warm year-round. They have rainy seasons and long dry seasons. Typically, individual trees are scattered across the landscape.

TEMPERATE GRASSLANDS (Prairies, Plains, Steppes, Veld, Pampas, Puszta) — Temperate grasslands have cold winters and hot summers. Trees grow along rivers and streams.

MOUNTAIN GRASSLANDS (Highlands of Tibet, the Andes, the Caucaucus and South Africa) — Mountain grasslands are cold, treeless plateaus near mountain ranges.

Find lessons on grassland animals in this book, *Draw•Write•Now®, Book Eight.*

Tundra Biomes

ALPINE TUNDRAS (Snow-capped mountain ranges) — Alpine tundras are the snow-covered meadows and valleys above the treeline. After the snow melts in the spring, small plants, mosses and lichens quickly sprout.

ARCTIC TUNDRAS (Siberia, Far North) — Arctic tundras are the lands that surround the Arctic Ocean and the North Pole. Arctic tundras have long, cold winters. The land is covered with snow and ice. In spring, the snow and ice melt and small plants, mosses and lichens quickly sprout.

Find lessons on the Arctic tundra, Antarctica and a map of Antarctica in *Draw•Write•Now®, Book Four.*

Shrub Land Biomes

SHRUB LANDS (Mediterranean, Maquis, Chapparral, Matorral, Fynbos, Mallee) — Shrub lands have hot, dry summers and rainy, warm winters. Tough, small-leafed shrubs with deep tap roots are capable of surviving the droughts.

■ Shrub Lands

Continents

Oceans

Find lessons on land biomes, freshwater biomes and saltwater biomes in *Draw•Write•Now®, Book Six.*

Desert Biomes

HOT DESERTS (Sahara, Australian, Chihuahuan, Mohave, Arabian, Kalahari and more) — Hot deserts are near sea level. Hardy small-leafed plants are typical. Cacti grow in North America and South America.

COLD DESERTS (Gobi, Great Basin, Atacama, Patagonia, Takla Makan, Turkestan and more) — Cold Deserts are located in high elevations. Snow falls on the land in winter, the sun scorches it in summer. Hardy small-leafed plants are typical.

Find lessons on desert animals in this book, *Draw•Write•Now®, Book Eight.*